DATE DUE

FEB. 4 1983			
MAR. 2 0 1984			
NO 25 '91			
FE 24 '92			
DE 04			
JE 21			

FAMOUS NAMES IN SPACE EXPLORATION

PAUL CLARK

Wayland

Other books in this series

Famous Names in Medicine
Famous Names in Crime
Famous Names in Science
Famous Names in World Exploration
Famous Names in Music
Famous Names in Sport

ISBN 0 85340 550 6
© Copyright 1978 Wayland Publishers Ltd
First published in 1978 by
Wayland Publishers Limited,
49 Lansdowne Place, Hove,
East Sussex, BN3 1HF, England
Printed by Cahills, Dublin

CONTENTS

JULES VERNE
creator of science fiction

Long before man could fly in the air, let alone in space, many imaginative writers thought of ways it could be done. Jules Verne made these wild ideas seem possible.

The son of a lawyer, he gave up studying law to write, at first for the theatre. Then he wrote a series of fantastic adventure stories starting with *Five Weeks in a Balloon* in 1863. *Journey to the Centre of the Earth*, the next book, is still popular with people of all ages and has been filmed. His exciting stories are set in unusual places—under the sea, in the air, and inside volcanoes. People in the nineteenth century were very keen on science. Verne was not a scientist but he understood scientific laws. He described things carefully and made them seem vivid and real.

Verne told stories of things which years later actually happened. It was as though he could see into the future. For example, *From the Earth to the Moon* gives the first realistic description of space flight. Three daring explorers are fired to the Moon in a giant cannon. Verne realized that they would need to go very fast to escape from the pull of the Earth's gravity. He estimated this speed, known as escape velocity, at 40,000 kph (25,000 mph). His estimate was correct. He had to put a cannon in his story, because it was the only machine that could launch something so fast. In fact, the passengers would have been flattened by the shock of the acceleration on firing. Otherwise, Verne's description of weightlessness and the take-off was very accurate. This book was a best-seller—some readers thought it was true! *From the Earth to the Moon* leaves the space explorers in orbit around the Moon, and its sequel, *Around the Moon,* tells of their return to Earth. In particular, the description of splashdown is very similar to those of the Apollo missions. The whole trip is similar to the *Apollo 8* mission of 1968.

After this first space adventure came many other exciting stories, sixty-four in all, including *Twenty Thousand Leagues Under the Sea* and *Around the World in Eighty Days.* His books have been translated into many different languages, and several made into successful films. Jules Verne laid the path for science fiction writers, and inspired many inventors who turned his fiction into fact.

KONSTANTIN TSIOLKOVSKY
father of the space age

It was 1903, the year the Wright brothers flew the world's first successful aeroplane. A deaf forty-six-year-old Russian schoolteacher brought out a book which laid the foundation of space science. It was called *The Exploration of Cosmic Space by Rocket*—and was written by Konstantin Tsiolkovsky. The man was a remarkable prophet.

He described, for the first time, how it would be possible to get enough thrust with a liquid-fuelled rocket to escape the pull of the Earth's gravity, and venture out into space. (Before his time, rockets were only of the firework type fired with solid chemical fuel.) He explained that an airtight craft would be necessary if humans were to travel in the vacuum of space. There was also the problem of escape velocity. He made suggestions for fuels, and showed how it was possible to reach these speeds.

His ideas did not bring him success overnight. An attack of scarlet fever had left him deaf at the age of nine. This made him lonely and withdrawn, and books became his friends. He taught himself enough maths and physics to study at Moscow Technical School. Later he became a schoolteacher near his home town, but he was thinking far into the future. He had some marvellous ideas. In 1892 he designed a special metal balloon called a dirigible and an aeroplane. He tested his models in Russia's first wind tunnel, which he designed and built himself. The authorities turned down his plans. So he turned his mind towards space travel, and in 1895 wrote a story which was first to describe a space station. It was not until after World War I and the Russian Revolution that his ideas caught on. Then he was given the praise and respect he deserved. They called him 'Father of the Space Age', and used his ideas in the rocket experiments of the 1920s and 1930s.

ROBERT GODDARD
true rocket pioneer

People laughed at the shy schoolmaster. They called him 'the moon rocket man'. Yet his inventions, ignored by the authorities at the time, are still used in rockets today.

Robert Goddard was hooked on space travel when he read *The War of the Worlds* by H G Wells as a boy. Like Tsiolkovsky, he was a teacher; he was also a good engineer. Despite bad health, he pioneered work that made rocket flight possible. Goddard wrote an historic pamphlet called *A Method for Reaching High Altitudes* in 1919. The main problem with rockets at the time was fuel. Goddard tried many fuels and engines and at last he launched the world's first liquid-fuelled rocket in March 1926. He used liquid oxygen as an oxidant, and petrol (gasoline) as a fuel.

This breakthrough made Goddard famous—and then people began teasing him. One man who took it all seriously was the great solo aviator, Charles Lindbergh. He took up Goddard's ideas and helped him get a grant of 50,000 dollars. This was just what he needed! With this money he could build larger rockets which could carry instruments. He improved the mechanisms, like fuel pumps, firing chambers, and guidance and recovery systems. In all he took out 214 patents.

By 1935 his rockets were reaching a height of 2,200 km at speeds of 885 kph. No rockets went as well as this until 1942, when the German V2 was developed. The authorities still did not see how vital his work was. When World War II began in 1939 his work ended, and soon after he died. In 1960 the US Government realized their mistake. They bought his patents for 1,000,000 dollars, and use his ideas to this day.

On the right, Robert Goddard stands beside the launching platform which holds his liquid oxygen and petrol (gasoline) rocket. This was on 16th March, 1926. The photograph was taken by his wife who helped him in his work.

HERMAN OBERTH
From the motor car
to the Moon in one lifetime

Herman Oberth is one of the few rocket pioneers who has lived to see his wildest dreams come true. He was born in a backward corner of eastern Europe, in Transylvania. There was no electricity or telephone and he did not see a motor car until he was ten! People thought his ideas for space travel were crazy—but he has lived to see them proved wrong.

At the age of twelve he read Jules Verne's *From the Earth to the Moon.* It fascinated him, even though he doubted if Verne's giant cannon would work. He studied medicine but also worked on possible means of space travel. After World War I he went to Germany, to talk to the government about liquid-fuelled rockets. No one was interested. He wrote about space travel for his exams at Heidelberg University, but his work was rejected as being too fanciful. It became the basis of his famous book *By Rocket to Interplanetary Space* published in 1923. This book became the source of all modern rocket theory. He showed how a rocket's flight could be worked out, if its fuel and size were known. He had lots of amazing ideas like telescopes mounted on space stations and multi-stage rockets like those used today. He was sure that man would fly in space in the near future.

Many people were excited by his ideas but other scientists thought he was a crank. Upset, he went back to Transylvania and became a schoolteacher. In the meantime the space craze was spreading. In 1927 a group of space enthusiasts formed the "Society for Space Travel" in Breslau, Germany. It grew rapidly. Oberth returned, joined the Society, and in 1928 became its president. The Society carried out many historic experiments with a variety of rockets.

Oberth had to work for the Nazis during World War II. After the war he worked on rocket fuels for the Italian Navy. Finally he was asked to go and work in the USA with Wernher von Braun on the US Army's rockets. He has now lived to see man reach the Moon.

The picture on the left shows Oberth at the age of sixty. He is an honorary member of the British Interplanetary Society, Honorary President of the German Society for Space Research, and winner of the R E P Hirsch Prize of the French Astronomic Society in 1929.

SERGIE KOROLEV
Russia's rocket genius

For many years the Russian space programme was secret. Now we know that much of their success in the 1950s and 1960s was due to one man—Sergie Korolev. He was the man behind the world's first artificial satellite, *Sputnik 1.* When it was launched, all the world was surprised—and the Americans were shocked! If the Russians could send up a satellite they could also send a nuclear warhead thousands of kilometres.

Korolev became interested in aircraft first. As a student he made his own glider, and in 1930 he joined a club of people like himself who were keen on rocket and space travel. Only two years later he was put in charge of the government-run Rocket Research Institute in Moscow. His work there was on rockets to launch gliders. These were later used in World War II to help aircraft take off. The Russians captured a number of German V2 weapons during the war. When it ended he led a team of scientists studying them. They built their own version, which was used for research into the upper atmosphere.

Korolev is pictured above with cosmonaut Herman Titov, and on the previous page with Yuri Gagarin.

In the early 1950s the Russians decided to build new large rockets that could be used for weapons and space research. They built a huge rocket launching site at Baikonur near Tyuratam in Kazakhstan. Here, Sergie Korolev worked on the new super-rockets. He designed very powerful rockets that could lift enormous loads. For the first time, it was possible to launch vehicles into space.

Korolev sent Laika the dog into space (see page 15) and was in charge of the early flights of Yuri Gagarin and Herman Titov. He helped design the space probes that went to Venus in 1961 and Mars in 1962. His team were also responsible for the first Russian communication satellite and the *Zond 3* mission which photographed the back of the Moon for the first time in 1965. Korolev died in 1966 and then the Russians revealed that he had been their Chief Designer of Spacecraft. His death was a great loss to the Russian space programme.

LAIKA
and the other animals in space

The early space scientists had a big problem. How would our bodies cope with being in space? Could we live in weightless conditions—and what would happen during blast-off? They could test the effects of acceleration in special centrifuges but it was hard to research weightlessness on Earth.

One solution to the problem was to send animals up in space. Before sending humans up, various creatures were

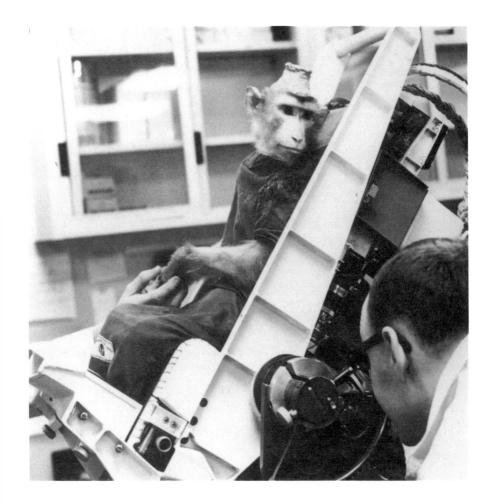

used in experiments. The Russians mainly used dogs, the Americans used monkeys and chimpanzees. They were checked like astronauts in training. The animals' health was carefully watched, and their reactions to the conditions and tests were recorded.

Laika became famous on 3rd November, 1957, when the Russians told the world that their second Earth satellite contained a living dog. Laika was sent up in *Sputnik 2,* and was the first living creature to orbit the world. On the ground the Russians kept a close check of her biological condition by radio signals. *Sputnik 2* was not designed to return to Earth and Laika died in space. Her last meal was poisoned, to prevent unnecessary suffering by suffocation. She was followed in August 1960 by Belka and Strelka who were brought back to Earth alive and well. Strelka later gave birth to six healthy puppies. In December 1960 Pchelka and Mushka went into orbit but died when their capsule burnt up on re-entry through the atmosphere. More tests were made shortly before Yuri Gagarin's flight. Russian scientists decided that humans could withstand the strains and stresses of space travel. In the USA, three months before John Glenn's flight, a chimpanzee named Eno was sent into orbit. US scientists agreed with the Russians that humans could survive in space. All space explorers owe a debt to the creatures who took the first steps into the unknown beyond the Earth.

Above, Laika sits in her special seat. On page 16 is a pigtail monkey used by the Americans for space research.

YURI GAGARIN
the first man in space

He flew in space for only 108 minutes, and orbited Earth just once. But Yuri Gagarin will always be remembered as the first man to fly in space.

Gagarin was a schoolboy when the Germans invaded Russia. His family had to flee, but survived, and after the war he went to technical school. Here he took up amateur flying and enjoyed it so much that he decided to become a pilot. As he was fit and was good at technical subjects, he was an ideal candidate for the Soviet Air Force, which he joined in 1957.

He was selected for the first group of cosmonauts in 1960 and underwent long and tiring periods of training. At last he was chosen to be the pilot of the world's first manned spacecraft, *Vostok 1.*

Yuri Gagarin speaks to the crowd at Sofia, Bulgaria.

On 12th April, 1961, Yuri Gagarin was launched into space from Baikonur Cosmodrome. The electrifying news that man had finally left the Earth flashed round the world! It was a space triumph for the Russians.

He returned to land by parachute and stepped out of his capsule, greeting the people who had watched him float down from the sky. In Moscow he was given a hero's welcome and met the Soviet leader, Mr Khruschev. He became a roving ambassador and visited many countries throughout the world. His pleasant manner and boyish good looks made him popular wherever he went. Gagarin spent several years training future cosmonauts, but was tragically killed in a flying accident at the age of thirty-four.

DR WERNHER VON BRAUN
top rocket engineer

It was the spring of 1945, during World War II. It was clear
that Germany was about to lose. Wernher von Braun, the
Germans' top rocket expert, chose to be captured by the
Americans rather than the Russians. Ever since his teens, von
Braun had dreamed of space travel, and in the USA his
dreams came true.

Dr Wernher von Braun, now Deputy Associate Administrator
of NASA, looks at the lunar TV camera which was used on
Apollo 15. That was the fourth manned lunar landing mission.

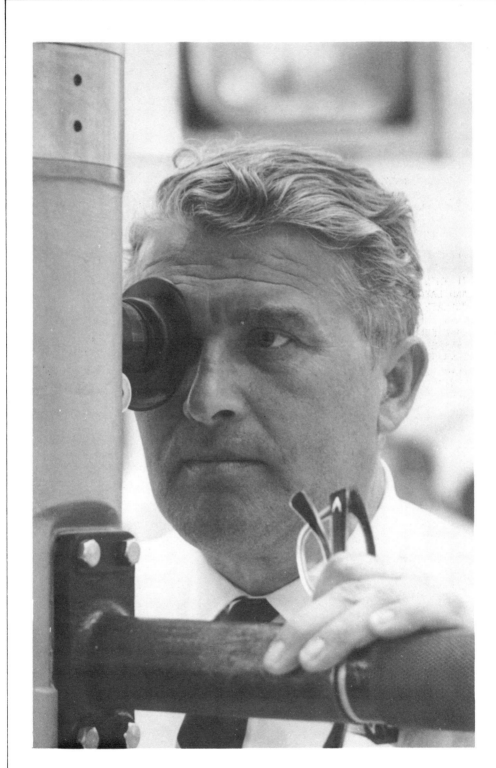

At eighteen he had joined the pioneer rocket society, the Society for Space Travel, of which Herman Oberth was a member. The German army soon spotted his talents—they wanted to develop new weapons. Von Braun was put to work to design large-scale rockets. In 1943 the Gestapo arrested him. They believed he was keener on space exploration than building weapons. Orders came from Hitler himself to release von Braun. He was vital to the success of the V2 rocket.

After the war, von Braun went to the USA and became a US citizen in 1955. He worked for the army and developed the *Jupiter C* rocket. This had been made for military use but von Braun saw it could be used to launch satellites. It put the first US satellite, *Explorer 1,* into orbit in 1958.

The Americans were stunned when the Russians put the first satellite, and then the first man, into space. So they decided to be first to the Moon. In 1961 President Kennedy announced that an American would go to the Moon and back by 1970! This was the huge five-billion-dollar Apollo programme organized by NASA, the National Aeronautics & Space Administration. Wernher von Braun was put in charge of the design of the huge three-stage *Saturn V* launch vehicle. It was the largest rocket that had ever been built. It weighed 3,000,000 kilos (3,000 tons) and produced a thrust of 3.4 million kilos (7.5 million pounds). It sent astronauts upwards at 40,000 kph (25,000 mph) in their Apollo spacecraft. The two dress rehearsal flights, *Apollo 8* and *Apollo 10* went perfectly—and in July 1969 a *Saturn V* rocket took the *Apollo 11* mission successfully to the Moon.

In the seven years of the Apollo programme von Braun's *Saturn V* rockets carried forty-five astronauts into space. Twelve set foot on the moon. All this happened without any loss of life. This was thanks to the vision and skill of a great man—Dr Wernher von Braun.

Left, Dr von Braun looks at the *Saturn I* space vehicle through a periscope in the launch control centre, just before launching. The vehicle was fired by a team from the NASA Kennedy Space Centre.

JOHN GLENN
America's first space hero

Like many space adventurers, John Glenn began as a pilot.
When at eighteen he told his parents that he wanted to be a
pilot, they were upset—they expected him to take over his
father's plumbing business. Ever since his school days he had
been obsessed with flying. He was very bright and athletic. He
was licensed to fly a civilian plane while still at college, and
when World War II began he joined the US Navy to train as a
fighter pilot. By 1945 he had flown fifty-nine missions against
the Japanese in the Pacific. When the war ended he stayed in
the Navy and learned to fly jet planes. Then in 1950 came the
Korean War. He had many narrow escapes; on one occasion
he returned from an air battle with over 200 holes in his plane.
Later he tested experimental planes, and broke the record for
crossing the USA in a jet. He did it in only three hours and
twenty minutes.

America was shocked by Russia's early space successes.
The Russians had put *Sputnik 1* and Laika into space. The
USA began 'project Mercury' in 1958 to get an American into
space. Seven experienced pilots, chosen from thousands,
trained as astronauts—one was John Glenn. The training was
very exhausting. It took great determination to keep going. On
20th February, 1962 he blasted off in his Mercury capsule on
top of an Atlas ICBM rocket. He orbited the earth three times.
He crossed the USA again—this time in eight minutes! He
became an instant hero after a good splashdown in the Pacific
Ocean but he never flew in space again. He received many
awards, including the Distinguished Service Medal from John
F Kennedy.

He passed on his experience by helping to train the next
generation of astronauts—those who would go to the
Moon.

Right, a smile of triumph from John Glenn on 21st February,
1962.

24

VALENTINA TERESHKOVA
the first woman in space

The Russians scored another 'first' in space when on 16th June, 1963 they launched a woman in *Vostok 6*. No American female astronauts will go into space until the 1980s when the space shuttle programme is under way.

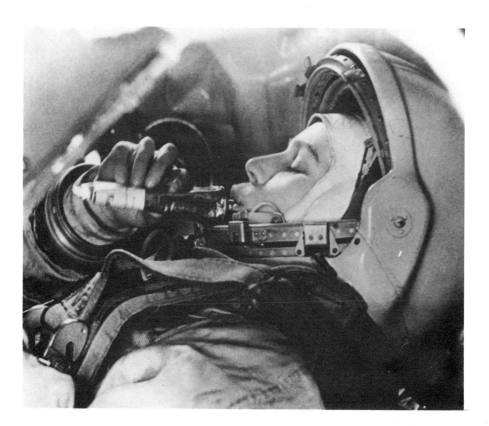

Valentina Tereshkova orbited the Earth forty-eight times, telling the world about the dramatic view she had of the Earth. Her biological condition and reactions to space flight were checked all the time. During the flight she suffered from space sickness and did not eat for three days. When she landed, peasant women gave her a meal of black bread and onions.

Tereshkova's father had died fighting in World War II and her mother had struggled to bring up three daughters alone. She worked in a textile mill with her mother and elder sister, and became interested in parachuting. She took up parachuting as a hobby and was awarded a 1st class certificate for skydiving by the Yaroslavl Air Club. Her balanced personality, strength and skydiving experience made her able to train as a cosmonaut at the 'Star Village' of Zvyezdni Govodok near Moscow. Here, she had to prove that she could stand the stresses of space flight as well as any man. She also had to learn all the complexities of space flight,

although she had no technical training. Her flight was a great success. Since then she has married Andrian Nikolayev, a fellow cosmonaut. Their daughter Elena is the only person to have both parents as space explorers.

Tereshkova's main job is still at the cosmonaut training centre, but she is also chairman of the Soviet Women's Committee. She travels to many countries as an ambassador of both the cosmonauts and the women of the USSR.

She is pictured above in Red Square with Valery Bykovsky, who was in orbit at the same time, in a separate spaceship.

SIR BERNARD LOVELL
a man who watches the universe

By looking up into the sky we can see distant stars. For centuries astronomers have studied them with telescopes, but as well as the light from the stars there are also radiations we cannot see. In the 1930s it was discovered that invisible radio waves also reach Earth from space. Scientists wanted to build radio telescopes to study this mystery. The telescopes are receiving aerials, large enough to pick up very faint signals.

Bernard Lovell worked on radar during World War II, helping to spot enemy planes. After the war he used army surplus radar gear to look carefully at meteors falling from space—with radar he could detect them even by day. He wanted to track the orbits of meteors, so he built a simple radio telescope. This was not enough. To study radio waves properly, a giant steerable radio telescope was needed. Where was the money to come from? Lovell launched a great campaign to raise enough backers—and the result was the famous Jodrell Bank radio telescope. It was finished just in time to pick up the 'bleep bleep' signal from *Sputnik 1*.

His telescope has since been used to track many satellites and manned space vehicles. Its main job, however, is to explore the depths of space, to pick up radio waves from millions of light years away. Some come from mysterious pulsars, and quasars. Pulsars are collapsed stars that have shrunk to a fraction of their original size. They spin and radiate energy in bursts. Quasars are baffling. They are incredibly remote in space, and give out large amounts of energy. This is one of the mysteries Lovell and his team still have to solve.

NEIL ARMSTRONG
the first man on the Moon

If ever a man deserved to be the first man on the Moon, it was
Neil Armstrong. From his early teens he lived for flying, and at
nineteen he joined the US Navy as a fighter pilot. During his
seventy-eight combat missions in the Korean War he had
many narrow escapes, which earned him a reputation for

being cool and tough. He always kept his head in emergencies and this saved his life several times. The big break came in 1955—he became a civilian test pilot for NASA, flying experimental rocket-powered aircraft such as the X-15. He flew higher and faster than any man before, up to 6,000 m and at 6,440 kph. His great flying skill, experience and enthusiasm made him a natural candidate for space.

In 1962 he started training with NASA as a civilian astronaut. His first taste of space flight came in 1966, when he piloted the two-man *Gemini 8* capsule. Two space vehicles joined up—the first docking manoeuvre in space. There was nearly a disaster when the spacecraft began to spin wildly but Armstrong brought it under control and made an emergency return to Earth. He was selected as command pilot for the *Apollo 11* Moon mission. In July 1969 the three-man crew set off for the Moon. Whilst Michael Collins circled the Moon in the command module, Armstrong and his co-pilot, Buz Aldrin, descended to the Sea of Tranquillity in the lunar module (LM). The planned landing site was covered with boulders, so Armstrong manually flew the craft six and a half kilometres further to make a safe landing. He took his place in the history books when, on 20th July, 1969, he became the first man to step on to the Moon. After setting out recording instruments and collecting Moon-rock samples the US astronauts made a faultless return to Earth. True heroes of the twentieth century, they were applauded throughout the world. They had done what some men had dreamed of—and others had thought impossible. Man had left the planet of his birth and set foot on our companion in space, the Moon.

Left, the crew of the *Apollo 11* moon-landing expedition pose in front of the Lunar Landing Module Simulator during their training programme. From left to right: Michael Collins, Neil Armstrong, and Edwin (Buz) Aldrin. The simulator is just the same as the real LM from which Neil Armstrong stepped onto the Moon on 20th July, 1969.

JAMES VAN ALLEN
and the belts around the Earth

The Earth is bombarded all the time by invisible particles from outer space, called cosmic rays. Our atmosphere protects us from most of these. In the 1930s and 1940s the only way to study them was to send special instruments up in balloons, but balloons cannot go above the atmosphere. A young scientist, James Van Allen, decided to use the German V2 rockets that the Americans had captured at the end of World War II. He designed special instruments that were light and did not take up too much room. He was good at doing this because during the war he had made fuses for artillery shells which also had to be very small. The rockets managed to get above the atmosphere, but only for a few minutes. Then they fell back to Earth.

By the late 1950s there were some much more powerful rockets, which had been developed for military purposes. Why not use them to put instruments into orbit in satellites? Van Allen and his team designed the equipment that went up in the first US satellite *Explorer 1* in 1958. Circling the Earth out in space, *Explorer 1* sent back information about the conditions there. The scientists were very surprised by the high level of radiation that the readings showed. Van Allen realized this was due to particles from the Sun being caught in the Earth's magnetic field. Later Explorer satellites plotted them accurately, and they are now called the 'Van Allen Belts'. We are normally protected from these radiations. Astronauts have to keep clear of them, or their bodies may be damaged.

Dr James Van Allen is seen here with a model of Jupiter and its radiation belts. Van Allen, who is based at the University of Iowa, USA, is quoted as saying, ''What use are Van Allen Belts? I make money out of them.''

CARL SAGAN
life on other planets?

For a long time, people have been fascinated by the idea that there might be other thinking beings somewhere in the universe. Carl Sagan believes that there are.

We do not know exactly how life began on Earth. We think that over millions of years simple gases were exposed to lightning. There were chemical changes and the result was a sort of organic 'soup' from which the first forms of life developed. It is very likely that the same thing could have happened on other worlds. Carl Sagan has made a mock-up in his laboratory which copies the conditions on a new planet. A mixture of simple gases like those on a new planet is exposed to ultraviolet light and electric discharges. The chemicals which result are organic compounds. Sagan and his team have found that these compounds exist on Jupiter. Many of the simple compounds necessary for life exist in space.

His work on Mars showed that germs (called bacteria) like we have on Earth could survive there, although it is much colder than Earth and has little atmosphere. When the Americans landed a probe on Mars in 1976, Sagan's equipment was on board to test for signs of life.

The American and Russian space probes found that the surface of Venus was very hot (900°C). Carl Sagan explained that this was due to a giant 'greenhouse' effect—the carbon dioxide atmosphere keeps in all the Sun's heat. He has suggested that the upper atmosphere could be 'seeded' with small plant organisms from Earth. Over a period of time they would make more oxygen, which we can breathe. This would allow the planet to cool and eventually man could live there. This sort of process probably happened on Earth millions of years ago. In 1976 Carl Sagan and his team made a message which beings on another planet may find. *Voyager 1* and *Voyager 2* space probes are flying past the giant outer planets.

When they leave the solar system they will travel out into interstellar space. The message, a collection of man-made and natural sounds, is recorded on a 30 cm copper disc. In thousands of years' time, a strange creature of another planet may find one and learn of our existence.

Another way to contact alien beings is to receive messages from them. Carl Sagan believes that we should 'listen in' to the universe for any messages that may be transmitted.

Carl Sagan, below, is now known to millions of people through his television talks about space exploration. He is Director of the Laboratory of Planetary Studies at Cornell University, USA.

GERARD O'NEILL
visions of the future in space

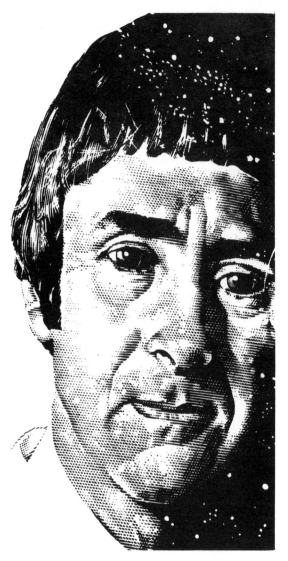

Gerard O'Neill is a scientist who sees a time, not far ahead,
when large colonies of people will live permanently in space.
He has written about these plans in his book *The High
Frontier.* There would be huge cylinders, like enormous tin
cans, or else spheres, holding about ten thousand people.

Some of the materials used to make them would come from Earth, but most would come from the Moon. The inside surface would be many kilometres square, and have forests, meadows and small villages. The climate would be carefully controlled, so that crops grew well and there was no pollution. It should be possible to create a balanced habitat, man-made instead of natural.

What would be the purpose of these 'islands in space'? If they stayed between the Sun and Earth, they could collect solar energy, the heat and light from the Sun, and send it back to Earth. Here on Earth we rely for our energy needs on fuels like oil, coal and gas which will one day run out. We are using up more and more, and the fuels are not being replaced. The Sun's energy is free and will not run out for millions of years. Making islands in space would be one way of solving our energy problems. They could travel far out into space, since the colonies would be self-supporting and never need to return to Earth. One day, 'space arks' could leave the Solar System and travel out through interstellar space. It would take thousands of years, but mankind could spread throughout the Galaxy.

Glossary

Acceleration   Rate of speed increase.

Aerial   Device for picking up energy from passing radio waves.

Astronaut   American term for space pilot or space scientist.

Artificial Satellite   Man-made package of instruments put into orbit around a planet or moon.

Atmosphere   The layer of gases around a planet. The atmosphere around the Earth includes oxygen which we need to breathe.

Bacteria   Microscopic single-celled organisms found almost everywhere on Earth. Some cause disease.

Centrifuge   Device used to simulate the effects of high acceleration.

Command Module   The spacecraft that circled the Moon whilst the Lunar Module descended to the Moon.

Communication Satellite   Satellite that relays radio and TV signals round the world.

Cosmic Rays   Very energetic atomic particles that rain on Earth from space.

Cosmodrome   Name given by the Russians to a rocket-launching base.

Cosmonaut   Name given by the Russians to space pilots or space scientists.

Dirigible   A powered and steerable balloon or airship.

Docking Manoeuvre   One vehicle joining up with another in space.

Escape Velocity   The speed necessary to leave the gravitational pull of a planet.

Firing Chamber   The part of the rocket engine in which the fuel and oxidant are mixed and ignited.

Galaxy   The large group of stars of which our Sun is a part. It is seen in the sky as the 'Milky Way'. There are many galaxies in the universe.

Gravity   The force that attracts all matter together.

ICBM   Intercontinental Ballistic Missile. Large-scale military rocket capable of carrying nuclear weapons thousands of kilometres.

Interstellar   Between the stars.

Light Year   Distance light will travel in one year. Used for describing vast distances in space. It represents 9.5 million million kilometres.
Liquid-fuelled Rocket   A rocket engine powered by liquid fuels. It can be controlled by turning them on and off.
Magnetic Field   Invisible lines of magnetic force that surround a magnetized object. The Earth acts as a gigantic magnet because its core is iron.
Meteors   Small solid bodies from outer space which burn up when passing through the Earth's atmosphere. Large ones may reach the Earth's surface.
Multi-Stage Rocket   A rocket vehicle of two or more parts. The lower, or main stage, lifts the other smaller stages before they are ignited. The main stage then drops away.
Nuclear Warhead   Very powerful weapon such as an atom bomb or hydrogen bomb carried on top of a rocket.
Orbit   The path of a body in space revolving around another, e.g. the path of the Moon around the Earth.
Organic   Containing hydrogen and carbon, essential to all forms of life.
Outer Planets   The large planets beyond the orbit of Mars.
Oxidant   Chemical (e.g. liquid oxygen) which burns with rocket fuel to produce thrust.
Radar   Very high frequency radio transmission and receiving equipment used to detect remote objects.
Radiation   An emission of rays or particles that are invisible to the human eye, e.g. X-rays.
Radio Waves   Electromagnetic wave motions that can travel through a vacuum.
Re-entry   The passage of a space vehicle through the atmosphere returning to Earth from space.
Science Fiction   Stories about things which might happen in the future.
Solar System   The planets, including the Earth, which revolve around the Sun.

Space   The universe which lies beyond our atmosphere.

Space Probe   Unmanned spacecraft carrying instruments, sent to investigate outer space

Space Station   Large artificial satellite that may be occupied by people.

Splashdown   Landing of spacecraft in the sea after return from space.

Sputnik   Russian name for their first series of instrument satellites.

Thrust   The pushing force developed in an aircraft or rocket engine.

Upper atmosphere   The top part of the atmosphere on the border of space above thirty kilometres.

Vacuum   Space containing no air or other gas.

Vostok   Name given by the Russians to their first series of manned spacecraft. It means 'East'.

Weightlessness   Effect that occurs in orbit when centrifugal force (the outward force of spinning) cancels out the downward pull of gravity.

Wind Tunnel   Device for testing aircraft designs in model form.

On the right, above, is *Skylab,* the first large orbiting space station. It enabled the Americans to carry out many important experiments in space, and to photograph the Earth extensively. It is likely that the Russians will establish permanent space stations in the near future.

On the right, below, is a proposal for a space-shuttle. The space-shuttle which the Americans will fly into space in the 1980s is the next step in space travel. It is re-usable, taking off like a rocket and returning like an aeroplane, which keeps costs down. It will be used for many different experiments in space. The Americans have invited people form other countries to use it. There will not be so many famous names in the future of space exploration as more and more work is the result of joint effort and large research teams.

Date Chart

the landmarks of space exploration
from powered flight to the Moon landing.

1903 The Wright brothers make first controlled flight at
     Kitty Hawk, USA
     Tsiolkovsky publishes *The Exploration of Cosmic
     Space by Rocket* in USSR
1919 Goddard publishes *Method of Reaching Extreme
     Altitudes* in USA
1923 Oberth publishes *By Rocket to Interplanetary Space*
     in Germany
1924 Society for Study of Interplanetary Communication
     founded in USSR
1927 Society for Space Travel founded in Germany
1928 Goddard launches first liquid-fuelled rocket (USA)
1930 Interplanetary Society founded in USA
1933 Interplanetary Society founded in Britain
1939 First flight of jet-powered aircraft (Germany)
1941 First flight of rocket-powered aircraft (Germany)
1942 First flight of V2 (Germany)
1944 V2 flies up to height of 190 km (118 miles)
     (Germany)
1947 Breaking of the sound barrier (332 mps / 760 mph)
     by rocket-powered aircraft (USA)
1957 First artificial Earth satellite put into orbit (USSR)
     Laika first living creature to orbit the Earth (USSR)
1961 First man to orbit the Earth, Yuri Gagarin (USSR)
1963 Valentina Tereshkova, first woman to orbit the Earth
     (USSR)
1964 First pictures of Mars from *Mariner 4* (USA)
1965 Aleksey Leonov first man to 'walk' in space (USSR)
1966 First 'docking' of two space vehicles (USA)
     First 'soft landing' on the moon by *Luna 9* (USSR)

1967 First death in space—Vladimir Komorov (USSR)
1968 First manned flight around the Moon—*Apollo 8* (USA)
1969 First men on the Moon, Armstrong and Aldrin from *Apollo 11* (USA)

Reading List

The Observer's Book of Manned Spacecraft by Reginald Turnhill, published by Warne in 1973.
The Observer's Book of Unmanned Spacecraft by Reginald Turnhill, published by Warne in 1974.
Space Magpie by Peter Fairley, published by Jackdaw Publications in 1977.
The How and Why Book of Planets and Interplanetary Travel published by Transworld Publishers Limited in 1976.
A-Z of Space by Peter Fairley, published by Hart Davis in 1976.
Rockets and Satellites by David Hardy, published by World's Work Limited in 1976.
Man and Space by Arthur C Clarke, published by Life Science Library in 1967.
Man's Future in Space by Patrick Moore, published by Wayland in 1978.

Picture Acknowledgements

Associated Press 9, 10, 35;   BBC 37;   David Baker 16;   Camera Press 19, 20, 21, 26, 27, 28, 29, 30, 31, 32, 38, 39;   Mary Evans 5; Keystone Press 17;   NASA 22;   Novosti Press Agency 6, 7, 12, 13, 15, 18;   Popperfoto 25. Other pictures are from the Wayland Picture Library.